1

Toolkit #6

# 10 Key Strategies for Responding to Disasters

Readiness, Response and

Rejuvenation of Your Nonprofit

Marilyn L. Donnellan, MS

# 10 Key Strategies for Responding to Disasters

ISBN 9798632623766

**Nonprofit Toolkits:**

Toolkit #1: Volunteer Handbooks
Toolkit #2: The Top Twenty Sustainability Strategies for Nonprofits
Toolkit #3: Becoming a Tech-Focused Nonprofit
Toolkit #4: ED Succession Plans and Search Process
Toolkit #5:  Developing and Marketing a Story-Telling Budget
Toolkit #6:  10 Key Strategies for Responding to Disasters

## Published by Kindle Direct
## ©2020, by Marilyn L. Donnellan, MS, Author

# Table of Contents

## Introduction

The pandemic hit the United States in early 2020 like a runaway freight train. By mid-March, every sector in every state felt the impact. Unemployment rates, particularly within the service industry, skyrocketed as restaurants and retail stores closed their doors and sent employees home. Nonprofits scrambled to figure out ways to continue serving their vulnerable populations: the elderly, children, disabled, hungry, homeless, substance abused and mentally ill. Health care workers were faced with shortages of essential equipment. Many of them fell victim to the pandemic while trying to help their critically ill patients. Seniors were separated from their loved ones to protect their health. Businesses of all types and sizes were forced to figure out new ways of doing business to prevent them from becoming economic victims. Centers of worship shut their doors and conducted services online rather than expose their parishioners to the virus.

The media and politicians struggled to keep up with the world-wide economic impact and to keep citizens from panicking. Online blogs and websites proliferated with not always accurate information on how the virus spread and what the responses should be.

What is it which made this pandemic disaster such a huge impact on everyone, much more so than just about any disaster? And what can we do to mitigate the results and help the nonprofit sector survive and thrive? What strategies do your nonprofit staff and board need to implement to continue achieving the vision, mission and strategic goals despite a disaster? How do we focus on our clients' needs and adapt what we do?

This toolkit will focus on ten keys to turn any disaster into opportunities:

1. Disaster response plan implementation
2. Review risk management plan
3. Implement sustainability strategies
4. Decide if outsourcing is an option
5. Develop adaptable training methods
6. Change programs to meet needs
7. Streamline administration
8. Create new resource development strategies
9. Focus on brand identity to implement marketing plans
10. Be nimble in responding to a disaster

Maintaining a positive attitude as you adapt to the changing environment caused by any disaster is necessary. John A. Call wrote in *Psychology Today,* "Learn to take challenges as they come, and think positively about the outcome of the situation. You will be able to overcome obstacles more easily with a more positive attitude."

## Defining a Disaster

All disasters are characterized by certain similarities:

- Sudden and unexpected
- Causes great damage and/or loss of life

Even with these characteristics, a disaster's impact can be reduced by preparedness. But how do you prepare for an unexpected event? The first step is understanding disaster impacts.

Nonprofits are particularly vulnerable to disasters because in their effort to be financially lean, disaster preparedness is relegated to the if-we-have-time-and-money category. Unfortunately, it is that type of thinking which makes any disaster's impact balloon for the organization, the board, staff, clients, volunteers and donors.

To better understand how your nonprofit is impacted by the current or future disasters, look at Fig. 1. The six key functions or core elements of a nonprofit clearly illustrate where the vulnerabilities are:

1. Administration
   - Accounting – ability to receive and process donations, payroll checks, vendor payments, outsourcing issues
   - Facilities, equipment – access to the facility; destruction or replacement; outsourcing of building and property maintenance; security issues
   - Technology – cybersecurity, access to computerized information, back-ups of

data; ability of communication systems to deal with increased volume of calls or emails; need to outsource telecommunications; purchase and installation of off-site technology

- Personnel – unemployment, working from home; off-site supervision issues; training on off-site equipment, updates to software; job duties changed; psychological issues
- Legal issues – permits needed for a different way of implementing programs, criminal background checks, bylaws changes

2. Board and volunteer development
    - Crisis communication policies and procedures
    - Implementation of a disaster plan (external and internal)
    - Specialized training of board members and volunteers in disaster response (external and internal)
    - Roles of board members and volunteers in dealing with the disaster
    - Adapting the strategic plan to environmental changes
    - Development or updating of a risk management plan
    - Emergency policies needing approval

3. Marketing
    - Crisis communication with the media
    - Impact on brand identity and marketing strategies

4. Programs
   - Access to clients
   - Continuing, eliminating or changing programs to an off-site approach
   - Funding of off-site program strategies
5. Community involvement
   - Role of the nonprofit in external disasters
   - Memorandums of understanding with emergency responders
6. Resource development
   - New strategies for raising funds and other resources
   - Role in helping other nonprofits.

And, finally, consider the disaster's impact on implementation of all aspects of the vision, mission and strategic planning goals of your nonprofit. How to adapt the plan to the changing environment can be confusing and frustrating for everyone.

But, when we work together and are willing to adapt to our new normal, we can change a disaster into multiple opportunities.

# Fig. 1: Core Elements of a Successful Nonprofit

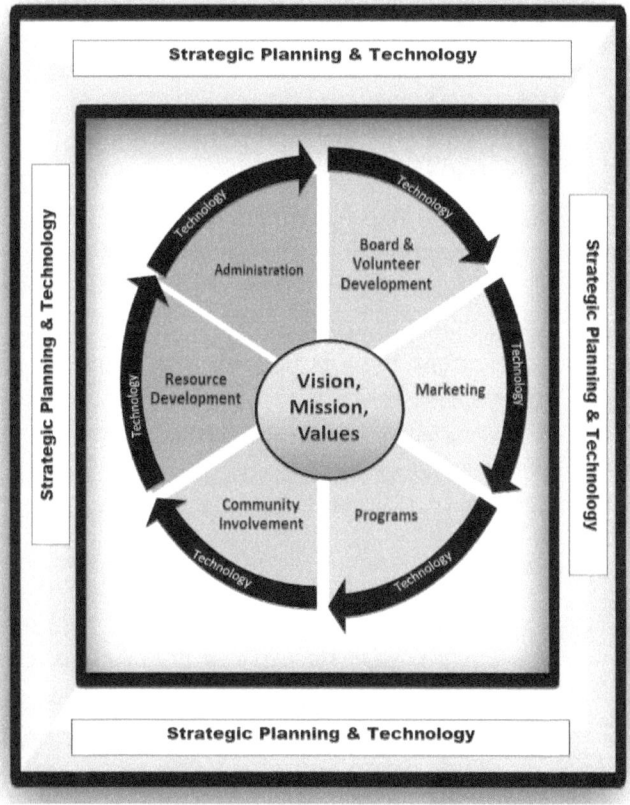

*Key #1*

# Develop or Update Your Disaster Response Plan

Unfortunately, too often nonprofits put off developing things like risk management and disaster plans, waiting for things to "slow down," or they have enough left-over funding. Bad idea.

The questions below are examples of the kinds of policies and procedures you need to develop and implement, even if you are in the middle of dealing with a disaster.

- Crisis Communication Policy: Who will speak to the media on behalf of the nonprofit?
- Crisis Communication Procedures: How will the board determine what will be said to the media?
- Internal Disaster Policies: Who decides when something is an internal disaster?
- Internal Disaster Procedures: How will you handle internal operations or administration if the facility is damaged (accounting, facility, technology, equipment, personnel, legal)? If you are forced to operate remotely, which administrative duties will be handled remotely, and which will be outsourced? If all staff will work remotely,

how will they be supervised? Who will train them in using remote equipment (computers, phone systems, etc.) How will all six of the core elements (Fig. 1) be impacted and revised? Will insurance cover any damages? What aspects of the risk management plan will be implemented? (Key #2) How will you prevent looting and secure the building?

- External Disaster Policies: Who decides what roll your nonprofit will assume to assist with the community disaster?
- External Disaster Procedures: Do you need to shelter in place? What types of disaster are most common in your geographical area and how will you respond to each? How will your nonprofit assist the community? Are memorandums of understanding needed to work with emergency responders? How will assisting the community impact your nonprofit's mission and vision? Are there liability issues? What aspects of the risk management plan will be implemented? How will volunteers and staff be trained? How will all six of the core elements (Fig. 1) be impacted by the external disaster?

These questions are just the tip of the proverbial iceberg when it comes to disaster readiness and response. Check with your county's emergency management agency and relief agencies like The American Red Cross on how to prepare and respond to all types of disasters.

*Key #2*

# Determine Impact on Your Risk Management Plan

Risk management plans encompass all aspects of the nonprofit before and after a disaster. These are a few of the primary areas to consider.

## Risk Management Audit

Audits of every aspect of risk can be very helpful, before, during and after a disaster. That's because a careful review of everything which could harm your nonprofit mitigates the impact on the vision and mission. Addendum D is a sample list of the risk issues which are especially important when responding to a disaster. By listing the issues in a checklist format, it is easier to see what you need to do. Add columns for cost to verify any expenses related to the issue are included in the budget or can be taken from the contingency fund in an emergency.

## Risk Management Committee or Task Force

Small nonprofits will benefit by the establishment of a risk management committee. The committee can review draft policies and procedures and make recommendations to the board (policies) and executive director (procedures). In Fig. 2 is an example of a board standing committee structure. In this case, risk management is delegated to the Administration Committee, and could function as a short-term task force if needed.

## Fig. 2 – Committee Structure

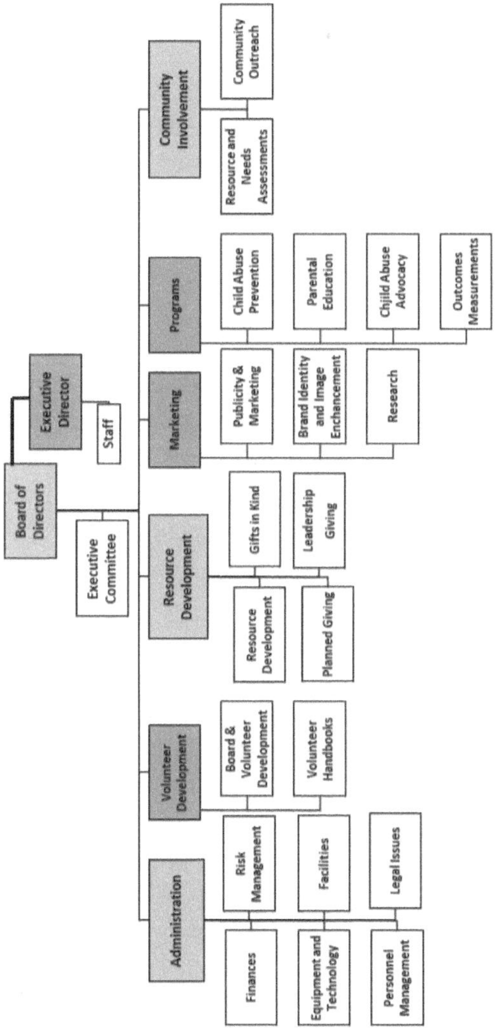

Insurance

Determine what insurance coverage you have related to liability issues: theft, disasters, cybersecurity, board and staff bonding, etc. Some companies offer insurance to cover salaries and wages during a disaster or sudden economic downturn resulting in a layoff. Check with your agent(s) to be sure you understand what coverage you have and do not have.

Abuse

Even if your employees are working off-site and you are offering on-line programs, know what types of policies and procedures are in place to prevent bullying, abuse and sexual harassment. Just because everyone is working off-site, doesn't mean they cannot be harassed or abused by callers. Know how to handle it if it occurs and instruct employees and volunteers on how to recognize abuse and report it. If the supervisor is the abuser, do you have whistle-blower policies to protect the employee who reports them?

Cybersecurity

Cybersecurity is not something to address only when you are hacked. It is not a question of if you will be hacked but when. And offsite use of technology to handle accounting, banking, programs, and donations can open you up to hacking and data breaches, unless you prepare for it. Your nephew is probably not the right person to handle cybersecurity. Hire a professional to test your systems and be sure you have as many firewalls as possible. Store important and sensitive data on the Cloud to reduce access. Change passwords frequently and make sure every off-site employee's computer, phone and tablet are protected.

Health and Safety

The pandemic is a wake-up call when it comes to safety of all constituents involved with our nonprofit. Hopefully, we all learned some valuable lessons about social distancing, washing our hands and disinfecting surfaces.

Think carefully before allowing volunteers and staff to return to the workplace after a disaster like a pandemic. To protect everyone, it is important to have every surface of your facility disinfected and cleaned before allowing anyone to return to work.

Other types of disasters require different safety protocols. Talk to an emergency management staff or any relief agency for suggestions.

Internal and External Disaster Plans

Verify you have policies and procedures in writing for both internal (disasters directly impacting your nonprofit) and external (disasters impacting the community) disasters.

Policies for internal disaster plans should include things like:
- How the nonprofit will respond to disasters impacting your ability to achieve the mission and serve clients
- The plan has been reviewed by the local emergency management agency

- Staff and volunteers are trained on how to deal with an internal disaster and the chain of command
- Emergency supplies and equipment are stored on premises
- Emergency responders annually tour the facility to verify it is disaster ready
- Exit routes are clearly posted throughout the building
- Regular fire and safety drills are conducted
- Emergency telephone numbers for responders, staff, board and key volunteers are easily accessible
- Emergency numbers for client families are available for the appropriate individuals
- The nonprofit knows how to assess the impact of an internal disaster on the facility, programs, staff, clients and volunteers

Policies for external disaster plans could include:
- The role your nonprofit will play in community disasters
- Mutual aid agreements have been signed with emergency responders, outlining the nonprofit's role
- Volunteers and staff are trained by emergency responders on their duties
- The nonprofit knows how to assess the impact of the external disaster on the programs, staff, clients and volunteers

<u>Crisis Communication</u>
- Who is authorized to speak to the media on behalf of the nonprofit?
- Written procedures for determining what the message to the media will be

<u>Contingency Fund</u>
- How much is put into the fund annually?
- What should be the maximum amount in the fund?
- Who is authorized to access the fund?
- When the fund can be accessed?
- How will investments of the fund be handled?

As this partial list illustrates, developing a useable risk management plan takes time and significant effort. However, having a plan before a disaster strikes will not only relieve the concerns of everyone involved with the organization, but will provide a road map for dealing with any type of disaster.

If you are currently dealing with a disaster, put together a disaster response team and brainstorm remotely on the areas listed here and decide which need to be implemented immediately.

*Key #3*
# Implement Sustainability Strategies

The ability of your nonprofit to cope with disasters is directly tied to the long-term sustainability strategies you have hopefully already implemented. Determine which need to be immediately implemented to help you through the crisis. Details on how to implement each strategy are included in the *Nonprofit Management Simplified* series and in the *Nonprofit Toolkits*.

### Sustainability Strategy #1
### Balance the Core Elements within the Infrastructure

Even if the disaster puts you into a crisis mode of operation, approach every strategy by carefully examining all the six core elements (Fig. 1). Be sure every emergency strategy you implement is evaluated based on the core elements. If your focus is entirely on programs, you could miss critical administration or internal operations issues on which programs are based. If you ignore fundraising because of the crisis, you could run out of money to serve your clients and achieve your mission. Balancing how you respond to each of the core elements as you deal with the crisis is essential.

## Strategy #2
### Establish a Clear and Transformative Vision and Mission

When you are in the middle of a crisis it is not the time to wonder if your vision and mission are valid. This is when you decisively implement your vision and mission.

## Strategy #3
### Embed Metrics across the Organization

If you have not already implemented metrics systems throughout your nonprofit, it will be more difficult for you to justify funding appeals during a crisis. Even in the middle of a disaster response, think about how you can translate what you are doing into measurable goals and objectives.

## Strategy #4
### Implement a Never-ending Strategic Planning Process

Hopefully, you have a strategic plan. Included in the plan should be disaster response goals. Without a plan and without disaster response policies and procedures, you will scramble to develop your response strategies. The award-winning Simplified Strategic Planning Process is a great tool, even in an emergency, to jumpstart your strategic plan. An overview of this proven strategy is now available as a one-hour webed (www.mldonnellan.com).

## Strategy #5
### Establish Outcomes Measurements

Like in strategy #3, it is difficult to implement a measurements system when you are dealing with a crisis. However, just because you haven't set up a research-based system to measure your programs' outcomes, add this to your list of things to do, even during a crisis. You will be better able to justify your requests for emergency funding.

### Strategy #6
### Build Relevant Programs

By adjusting your current programs to adapt to the crisis, you will be building relevant programs. If you set up a virtual tool for literacy programs, for example, you will be able to use the tool for home-bound clients after the disaster, too.

### Strategy #7
### Diversify Funding Sources

You have no choice. To adequately fund the changes in your programs during a disaster, you need different ways to raise funds. Fundraising events were not possible during the virus for fear of spreading the disease. If events are a significant source of funding for you, examine other strategies to raise funds.

### Strategy #8
### Evaluate Fundraising Costs vs. Fundraising Income

Be sure whatever funding strategies you implement (#7), always compare the costs for the strategy compared to the net income.

## Strategy #9
## Implement a Senior Staff Succession Plan and Policies

If any of your senior staff contract the virus or are impacted adversely by any disaster, can you immediately fill their position with qualified individuals? What about your own position as the executive director? Who will take over your job?

## Strategy #10
## Establish Institutional Memory Procedures

When we are dealing with a disaster is when it might hit us: "We don't have all of our nonprofit's history written down and our databases backed up off-site." Even if that is true, implement these procedures as quickly as possible.

## Strategy #11
## Implement Accelerating Technologies

Accelerating technology infers you have the best equipment needed to respond to the disaster. If you don't, you may have to scramble to get it in order to respond virtually to your clients and to conduct programs and all other functions remotely.

## Strategy #12
## Outsource What you Can

This is a key strategy if you are now having to operate remotely. It will be difficult to hire someone off-site to do your accounting if you are not already outsourcing it. This will be covered in more detail in Key #4.

### Strategy #13
### Implement a Volunteer Succession Plan

Just like in sustainability strategy #9, succession plans are needed for board members, officers and for key volunteer positions, like a special event. It is during a disaster when you may need to implement the succession plan. Be sure all volunteers understand how they can help.

### Strategy #14
### Establish Regular Board Training

If your board has not been trained in their legal governance responsibilities it will be more difficult to get them to act during an emergency. Fortunately, even last-minute training can be done remotely by using our webeds or by hiring a consultant experienced in virtual training.

### Strategy #15
### Recruit High-Capacity Volunteers

It is during emergencies you realize how important are highly experienced, very knowledgeable volunteers. If you have someone from The American Red Cross or a representative from the county's emergency management agency as a volunteer or serving on your board of directors, you will have first-hand information to help you through the crisis.

### Strategy #16
### Integrate Marketing throughout the Organization

Dealing with a disaster is tough enough without also having to figure out how to raise money or to get the word out on how your services are available. If relationships are already established with the media, it will make crisis communication easier.

## Strategy #17
### Demonstrate Value to the Community
And here is where your nonprofit should shine. It is during a disaster the nonprofit community always steps up to the plate to respond and provide services, usually long before any government services arrive. In most cases, demonstrating value will be easy if you adapt your needed programs to a different way of doing business. And, that will translate into funding.

## Strategy #18
### Build Competitive Advantage
Yes, we have competitors within the nonprofit sector. However, it is usually during a disaster we discover we are not so much competitors as collaborators in responding to needs. The question is, are you regarded as the community expert in your field, or is someone else? If you are not the leading nonprofit, be willing to set aside your ego and work together. Which brings us to sustainability strategy #19.

## Strategy #19
### Leverage Assets through Collaboration
Disasters provide a great opportunity to leverage your nonprofit's assets in collaboration with community responders to the disaster. What can you contribute to help mitigate the disaster?

## Strategy #20
## Establish Leadership Role in the Primary Mission

You are going to have a difficult time leveraging other nonprofits' assets if you are not the community leader in your primary mission. If you are not the leader, be willing to collaborate (#19) and be available to assist in whatever way you can.

These twenty sustainability strategies are important to your nonprofit's ability to continue providing services for the long term. When you are in the middle of responding to disaster, implement as many of these strategies as you can and begin now to figure out how you will implement all of them when things calm down.

*Key #4*
# Decide if Outsourcing is an Option

There are a wide range of options for outsourcing tasks, particularly during a disaster response. Before you outsource anything, get at least three bids from companies qualified to provide the service. Ask for references. Compare the cost to outsource with the cost to hire the staff qualified to perform the tasks, including the costs of benefits. Just be careful about how you do this. If you replace a staff position with a volunteer (even for outsourcing) you could be accused of unfair labor practices.

Accounting
Regardless of the size of your nonprofit, outsourcing your accounting makes sense because any CPA you hire is required by law to know the standards for nonprofit accounting.

Four out of the five nonprofits where I served as the CEO had significant financial management problems when I was hired. In every case, it was lack of knowledge of internal controls or fund accounting which led to the problem. Add into that mix board members who did not understand accounting enough to be able to ask the right questions and it led to preventable problems. One of the organizations had a $1.2 million deficit and the board did not realize it.

Outsourcing your accounting, before or after a disaster, usually makes good sense, especially for small nonprofits who may not have the funds to hire a qualified accountant.

It is possible to handle just about every accounting task remotely. Verify the vendor's computer security and how they keep records safe. Arrange for virtual deposits and payments. Compare costs for banking services with online platforms like PayPal.

## Facility

Whether you own or rent your facility, consider a property manager to handle upkeep inside and outside the building. Include in the contract how they will respond in an emergency. Landscape companies will often include emergency clauses for them to respond quickly to clear debris and fallen limbs on the property.

## Technology

Equal to accounting in importance is the security of your technology. If you have a contract with a technology company to remotely upgrade and solve computer problems, include an emergency clause to cover repairs and access to off-site computers when you are unable to access the facility, as in the pandemic.

Be sure anyone you outsource technology maintenance to has multiple fire walls to prevent cyber-attacks. This includes for any off-site computers.

## Personnel

A board member at my fourth nonprofit suggested I investigate outsourcing all the human resources (HR) management functions. I was skeptical. We only had four staff at the state association, and I had a degree in HR Management. I couldn't see how it would benefit the nonprofit.

However, after careful analysis, I was surprised to find outsourcing all personnel management and HR functions saved us money and prevented liability issues.

Because companies like ADP become the employer of record for all employees, you no longer deal with performance reviews, hiring and all labor laws. Those things become the responsibility of the HR management firm.

In an emergency, you will still need payroll functions off-site if your staff continue to be employed remotely.

Marketing and Resource Development

Choosing to outsource marketing and fundraising tasks, especially during a disaster, may not be financially viable. Always get at least three bids from different companies and compare their costs to having your staff do the same thing remotely. Small nonprofits (budgets under $1 million) may find outsourcing helpful. However, be very careful to examine the percentage of what the company raises goes into their pockets. Companies who specialize in raising money for organizations like police and firefighters are notorious for their extremely high costs. The result is the nonprofit may end up with less than 10% of the total money they raise.

Regardless of which tasks you outsource, do your homework before making recommendations to your board. During an emergency is not the time to make less than thoughtful decisions.

# Key #5
## Develop Adaptable Training

Although it is not often training is regarded as a key strategy for adapting to a disaster, it is in fact one of the most important and a great opportunity. Here is why.

If we are used to doing things in our nonprofit a certain way, when a monkey wrench, like a disaster, is thrown into our procedures we become confused and frustrated. Unless every stakeholder in your nonprofit is re-trained on how to fulfill their tasks, ineffectiveness will become the norm.

Think about it. Your facility is closed because of the disaster. Any work you will do to achieve your mission may have to be done off-site and probably by computer and telephone. But how many of your staff are properly trained to do this?

- Do they know how to use conference software like Zoom? What about your board members and volunteers, not to mention your clients who may need training on the new way of accessing services?
- What if your clients do not have computer access, how will you communicate with them? Do they know how to use smart phone technology like Facetime? Do they have access to a phone?
- How will donors get ahold of you if your website crashes from overuse?

- Are senior staff trained in how to do off-site, virtual supervision of their staff with a computerized project software?

Once you go down this training rabbit hole it is easy to become overwhelmed by the scope of the training needing to be done and done sooner rather than later if you are going to get ahead of the disaster curve.

Fortunately, computers and online platforms have made training much easier.

When the pandemic began to impact our consulting business, one of the largest clients, a national association, made the decision to cancel our on-site facilitation sessions to guide them in strategic planning. The bulk of the people who would be attending were no longer able to travel from their respective locations around the country to their headquarters in the Washington, D.C. area.

Fortunately, another client asked if we could do board training remotely a month before the virus became an issue. This gave us some experience in the process.

By switching to an on-line conference system which is sophisticated enough to allow us to set up small groups during the session, we not only protected our client and their participants, but we protected ourselves. Another bonus for the client was the reduction in costs; now they did not have to pay our travel costs. It was a win-win for everyone and worked very well.

Look at everything you do and decide what can be done off-site and what kind of training is needed and for whom. Fig. 3 is an example of a checklist you could develop to examine your training needs.

One way to look at this is to consider what you would need to do if you recruited a highly skilled person with a disability to do grant research for you. Your arrangement with them is for them to work from home since reliable transportation will be a problem because of their wheelchair.

Will the equipment and furniture they use be ergonomically correct? If it isn't will you be liable for any resulting health issues? How will you supervise them? Will the supervisor and the disabled employee need training on the use of headsets or specialized software?

Ask the same questions for all your training needs. Use this inquiry approach for every person working off-site. Establish on-line training times and train multiple staff and volunteers at the same time. Just be sure whoever is doing the training knows how to use whatever platform you choose for training. It might feel awkward at first, but with time you will find a lot of advantages to this type of training:

- You will be able to record the training and make it available to anyone unable to attend the initial training. Just be sure you are not violating any copyrights if you record the session.
- Once you become comfortable with the conferencing software, it can be used for board meetings, committee meetings, staff meetings, meetings with perspective funders, etc.
- For facilitation and training like board development and strategic planning, develop contracts or memorandums of understanding

with outside facilitators or consultants to clarify roles and expectations.

- Follow-up every training with an evaluation form (emailed or like Survey Monkey) to identify any glitches in the training.

Carefully examine ALL the six core elements (Fig. 1) to identify needed training to adapt to the changing environment in which you are operating. By the way, this type of on-line conferencing can work with clients, too, if there is a degree of computer knowledge and access to a computer with a camera and microphone.

Crisis lines, like 211, are very familiar with using teleconferencing and on-line platforms and will probably be helpful as you develop your new system.

If you are not comfortable doing the training yourself, hire a knowledgeable and experienced consultant. Often, the company selling you the equipment or software will offer free training, usually by on-line videos.

## Fig. 3 – Off-site Work Checklist

**Employee:** _____

**Supervisor:** _____

| Task | Software/equipment needed | Budget cost | Training required | Task Completion date | Special instructions |
|---|---|---|---|---|---|
| Research potential grants | Computer, headset, Printer, Office 365 | Computer: $500<br>Headset: $75<br>Printer: $200<br>Office 365: $350 | X<br>X<br>X<br>X | 9/17/2020 | Supervisor will check-in daily to make sure everything is working correctly |
| Submit list of potential grants to supervisor | Grant tracking software | Software: $300 | X | 9/25/2020 | List to only include funders which meet criteria |
| Write ten grants | Grant tracking software | Project management software: $200 | X | 1/5/2021 | Written submissions approved by supervisor before sending out |

*Key #6*

# Change Programs to Meet the Needs of Clients and the Community

Although training is essential for your new normal, adapting and changing your programs to provide essential services to your clients when you cannot meet with them face-to-face is often hard to do. Here is where flexibility and creativity are important. These two examples will help you make the changes:

1. Addendum A is a sample program evaluation form. Use this form to evaluate the current programs to see if they can be continued virtually or in a different location during the crisis.

2. Addendum B is like Addendum A, but the focus is on the crisis and how the nonprofit can react with each program.

Adapt these forms to your program needs, add relevant disaster response questions, or consolidate them into one form. Once forms have been completed for each program, take them to a board-appointed program committee (virtually if necessary) for their review. The committee will then take their final recommendations to the board for approval of the addition, elimination or temporary stop of any program.

At the heart of any decision must be the best interests of the clients. Maybe there is another nonprofit in your community better equipped to provide virtual services to your clients. Be willing to refer clients to them if they can accept the additional numbers.

Do you know the personal phone numbers and email addresses of your colleagues? Remember, they are probably in the same situation. Reaching out to them can be an encouragement to both of you.

Certain types of programs are more adaptable to virtual methods. A youth soccer program is difficult to conduct anywhere but on a soccer field. But, maybe the participants can play soccer games on their computers. Develop ways to make the virtual games learning opportunities. Have the youth submit to the coach any strategies learned from the virtual game and incorporate them into an on-line chat.

Programs like literacy are adaptable to computer use while programs geared to helping abused children and families are more difficult.

Think creatively. How can you use the computer and telephone to keep in touch with your abused clients?

If a client is in a domestic violence situation, how will you move her and her children to a safe shelter? Is the shelter open? Should the shelter move clients to motel rooms to protect them from the virus? How will you provide security to keep them safe?

Have an on-line brainstorming meeting with your staff to come up with creative solutions for client help and interaction.

Hopefully, you have a good working relationship with your community's information and referral center, 211 and/or crisis line. Keep them informed of changes in programs. This allows them to convey accurate information to anyone calling them for help or information.

The number one problem in any community, whether in a crisis or not, is not lack of resources but not knowing where the resources are. For the clients or other citizens in crisis from a disaster like the pandemic, being able to find and access desperately needed resources is critical.

Food banks, homeless shelters and other emergency services will be strained beyond their limits in a disaster. Be willing to share resources for the neediest residents and the nonprofits serving them. During and after a disaster is NOT the time to hoard or hide your resources but to share them.

Volunteers will still be needed, but maybe in a different way. Again, this is where your creativity comes to the forefront. Your telephone lines will probably need to be switched to an answering service. Maybe you can set up a bank of telephones (virtually), staffed with trained volunteers and connected through the answering service.

Look for ways to channel the outpouring of people wanting to help with those who need it while keeping everyone safe. There are a variety of ways to incorporate trained virtual volunteers into your disaster response.

Don't forget to include people with disabilities into your virtual volunteer pool. They are often highly experienced in coping with difficult times. It is estimated 20% of residents in every community are disabled. This is a huge untapped resource for your nonprofit, not only during a disaster but after. Fig. #4 gives you some examples of different types of duties disabled and virtual volunteers might do.

**Fig. 4– Examples of Virtual Volunteer Duties**

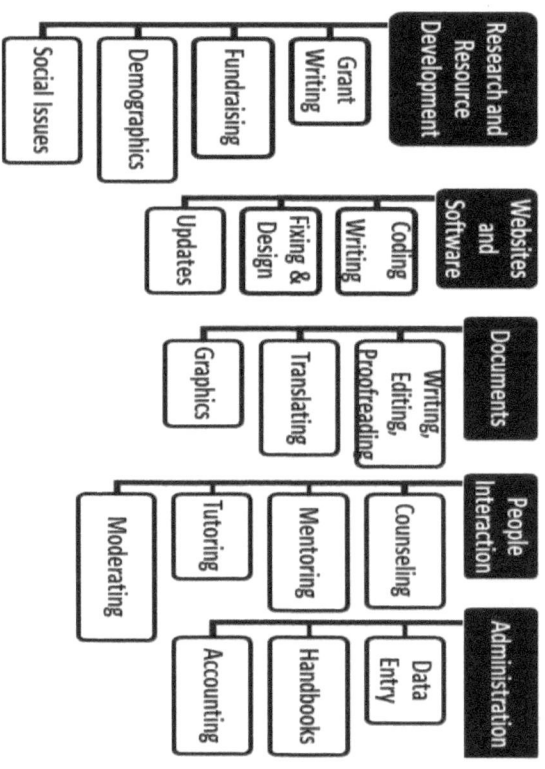

*Key #7*
# Streamline Internal Operations

For good or bad, disasters will often force you to streamline internal operations (IO) or administration down to only the essentials. How do you do that while still meeting basic standards of excellence for nonprofits?

Obviously, there are certain IO standards you must meet, regardless of the situation, such as accounting internal controls. Figuring out how to do that remotely can be a challenge, especially if your accountant cannot get into the office because of possible contamination or damage. There are several ways to do this:

- Accounting

  Forward all mail to the accountant's home if they will be working remotely. Be sure their computer system includes the right software to record accounts receivable (AR) and accounts payable (AP). Even use of Excel spread sheets to record AR and AP is better than nothing. Change from payment by check to electronic payments. Allow for direct deposit or through an on-line system like PayPal, which allows the accountant to receive and process donations, payroll checks, and make vendor payments. The accountant should be able to figure out ways to meet the rigid separation of duties issues.

If necessary, check into outsourcing all accounting functions (Key #4) temporarily to your auditor since they are already familiar with your accounting system.

- Facilities and equipment
  If access to the facility is not possible because the landlord has closed it, check to be sure security is adequate to protect your assets. Looters love disasters. Add a camera detection system or an alarm. If you own the building, hire a vendor to maintain the property and who will be available to clean the inside when staff is authorized to return.

- Technology
  Linkages between off-site computers is important, especially if you are going to continue running programs remotely. Be sure everyone involved has a secure computer and your cybersecurity policies and insurance will cover remote access. Verify each person working remotely has a back-up system and the ability to communicate remotely (speaker and camera). If someone will be handling calls, either use an answering service or make sure clients, volunteers, board members and media know how to get ahold of you. Train them on what you want them to say and do.

- <u>Personnel</u>
  If you are forced to close the nonprofit, notify employees with a personal call, not a heartless email or text. Be creative and look for ways to keep staff working from their homes. Determine if the new federal CARE grant might be a loan or grant source to keep employees on. Establish off-site supervision policies and procedures and determine ways to make sure everyone is trained on off-site equipment. If individual job duties change, revise job descriptions accordingly. Develop ways to communicate up-beat, positive messages. NEVER assume, just because the facility is closed, all employees need to be laid off. Look for creative ways to keep them busy and on the payroll.

- <u>Legal issues</u>
  Will you need any special at-home business permits? Consider all possible legal issues, especially if you will be offering remote programs. Will you need anyone to sign disclaimers or confidentiality statements? How will you make sure everyone working on-line with clients is not harassing, bullying or abusing clients? Will you still need criminal background checks? Verify there is nothing in your bylaws preventing you from working or serving clients off-site. If there is nothing in the bylaws about disaster response, talk to an attorney familiar with nonprofit law to find out if you need to make any bylaws changes.

All the internal operations and administration issues ensure your back-room operations continue to function properly. You may find the need to develop new policies and procedures for operating remotely.

Streamlining your internal operations procedures might end up being easier than raising needed funds.

*Key #8*
# Create New Resource Development Strategies

Disasters do not wait for you to raise enough money to deal with them. Therefore, having a six-months to a year contingency or reserve fund is vital. While you work to develop new ways of conducting programs and to keep the virtual doors open, develop new ways of raising the funds needed.

Addendum C includes some of the funding strategies which may still be viable while dealing with the disaster. Keep in mind that many of your past donors may be impacted by the disaster. Treat every donor and potential donor with compassion and respect.

Look for ways to do collaborative fundraising with like nonprofits or federated workplace campaigns like United Way.

Be creative. Think outside your restrictive box. A food bank was desperate to get additional funding during a downturn in the economy. They printed a message on brown paper bags, asking people to donate the equivalent of one paper bag lunch to the food bank. It worked better than anything they had tried before, primarily because it was so visual and relatable.

Heifer International is an expert at this type of fundraising. They ask people to donate one cow (or the equivalent in money) to a needy family. When donors learn how a cow can change a poor family's lives, it makes you want to buy more cows, pigs, goats or chickens.

Think about what makes you and your programs unique and turn that brand identity into fundraising.

*Key #9*

# Focus on Brand Identity to Implement Marketing Strategies

Nonprofits often think of brand identity as a negative because it is so prevalent in conversations about big business. And, "By gum," the nonprofit says, "we are not a business!"

However, if we remove the unfair stigma and realize it is local business that provides us with the funding to fulfill our mission, maybe we can look at branding as another tool in our marketing arsenal rather than a negative. Think of brand identity as the vision of the nonprofit, or the personality

Three potential brand identities are overviewed in the book, *Discipline of Market Leaders,* by Michael Tracey and Fred Wiersma. Although geared to for-profit business, I adapted the identities to the nonprofit sector. Think about these identities as you struggle to figure out how to do marketing in a disaster situation.

Operational Excellence

Nonprofits with this brand are striving to provide the best possible programs for the lowest cost and highest rate of efficiency and positive outcomes. During a disaster, if this is your brand, focus your marketing strategies on how efficient and effective you are in providing programs to victims of the disaster. The Salvation Army's substance abuse program is a good example of effective use of this brand identity.

## Program Leadership

The latest and greatest programs characterize this brand. Marketing strategies appeal to innovative, creative people. If you can come up with unusual ways to still provide effective programs to clients, regardless of cost, you will appeal to donors who are change agents and value creativity. Most youth programs are based on this brand.

## Client Intimacy

No matter how inefficient or costly it might be, nonprofits with this brand will do just about anything to provide services to their clients, even if they need to refer them to someone else. The health care profession is a vivid example of this, particularly during their response to the pandemic.

Revise your marketing plans to reflect the changes in your programs, your response to the disaster and how you are serving the community. If you do not have a marketing plan when a disaster strikes, you need to get one put together quickly. Consider asking for help from a local public relations or marketing firm. Many times, they will donate their time if they understand your brand identity and want to make a difference in the community, especially during and after a disaster.

*Key #10*

# Be Nimble in Responding to Disasters

Quick thinking and the ability to respond calmly to disasters is essential if your nonprofit is to survive and thrive. But what does that mean?

Being nimble is defined as "quick to comprehend," or "agile." These traits are a must when responding to the unexpected. Leadership is not about who is in charge, but who the followers choose to lead them.

Disasters bring out the best and worst in people. Looters take advantage of disasters to try and make a buck. Other people isolate themselves socially and physically to avoid having to deal with difficult situations.

As a nonprofit leader you have many people you are responsible for: your family, clients, staff, volunteers, board members, donors and even the wider community. To be a nimble leader you need to know ahead of time what are the policies and procedures you will follow if a disaster strikes. But it is more than following the plan. It is also about taking the initiative to adapt the programs and the internal operations to the changing environment. It is the ability to convince everyone involved what you are doing is the right thing to do.

Leaders do not stand around wringing their hands crying, "Woe is me!" Leaders get to work. They implement their well-thought-out plans and motivate others to do the same.

During the pandemic it was fascinating to watch how people reacted. Some hoarded toilet paper for who knows what reason. Others figured out creative ways to encourage their neighbors. Comedic reactions on Facebook to the ridiculous antics of hoarders helped to ease the tension we all felt.

A church in Florida, whose doors were closed to protect parishioners, implemented a drive by service. Anyone could drive by the church and be handed an encouraging Bible verse and a smile. In Italy, musicians serenaded apartment residents to lighten their day.

Residents serenaded their fellow residents in a locked down facility by spacing themselves six feet apart and singing hymns to residents who opened their doors.

Countless numbers of individuals quietly figured out ways to support their neighbors and still maintain the six-feet distance from each other.

As we sadly expected, politicians from both parties wrangled endless about critically needed economic assistance to citizens. They criticized anyone trying to get things done by saying it wasn't enough. Pet pork projects (or irrelevant projects) were tacked onto the funding bill, holding the bill and citizens hostage.

One politician emphatically intoned, "We need help now." But he never did say what help was needed, or how it was going to be paid for and disbursed. Instead, he blamed the workers in the trenches for not doing enough while he pompously pontificated. What was he doing to make things better? Who were the leaders? The politician or the anonymous workers frantically making face masks, or the beer brewery who switched from making beer to making badly need products for health care workers?  Or the health workers who worked long shifts to save peoples' lives while putting their own lives at risk because of inadequate equipment?

Regardless of where you are in developing or implementing disaster plans, consider all the key strategies listed in each chapter.  They are based on decades of experience preparing for disasters and implementing strategies.

## Addendum A:  Program Evaluation Form

**Person submitting the form:**

_____

**Date:** _____
**Program name:**

_____

**Rationale for the program (Vision or "Why" the program exists):** _____

_____

_____

**Mission (or "What" the program does):**

_____

_____

**Goal or Outcomes Measurement (How do you know the program is successful?):** _____

_____

_____

**Client Age Group:**

_____

**Number of Clients:**

_____

**Transportation Needs:**

_____

**Lead Staff:**

_____

**Number of Volunteers:**

_____

**Hours Program Offered:**

_____

**Location:**

_____

**Can Program be Conducted Virtually?** _____
**Why or why not?** _____

_____

**Annual Budget (per month):**
- **Expenses:**
- **Income:**

**Marketing Strategies:**

_____
_____
_____

**Legal or Insurance issues:**

_____
_____
_____

**List any challenges or threats to the program:**

_____
_____
_____

**Why should this program be started/continued or eliminated?** _____

_____
_____

**What will be the impact on clients if the program is discontinued or stopped for any length of time?**

## Addendum B:  Strategic Analysis Form

Answer all relevant questions and present a written report to the designated board-level committee for consideration.  Include a program plan (Addendum A) if the analysis is about a proposed addition, major change, or elimination of a program.
**Person submitting the report:**

_____

**Date:** _____

1.  How does the proposal or disaster challenge support our vision and mission or impact them?

2.  What are the leadership, volunteer, staffing or other personnel challenges?

3.  What are the operational implications?

4.  What are the expenses? (Include all staffing, implementation and facility costs, etc.)

5.  Where will the income come from to cover costs? (Include potential sources such as client fees, grants, etc.)

6.  What are the legal and insurance implications?

7.  What are the demographic rationales?

8.  What are the statistical reasons for the challenge or issue to be evaluated?

9. How will this issue impact our marketing and resource development strategies?

10. What are the competitive issues?

11. Are there are other nonprofits addressing the issue or challenge and how will our approach differ or enhance their efforts?

12. How will this issue impact our unique role in the community?

13. How will this issue or challenge impact our future growth?

14. How does this fit with our strategic plan and how will it change the strategic plan?

15. What are the positive and negative impacts of the issue?

16. What are the technology and equipment needed to conduct the program off-site or virtually?

17. What is your recommendation? (State in one sentence and include an outcomes measurement: How will we know we have addressed the issue?)

## Addendum C – Resource Development Strategies

| Strategy |
|---|
| **Crowd Funding:** An evolving strategy whereby the Internet is used to generate donations for specific causes, both short and long-term |
| **Direct Mail:** Solicitation of contributions through the postal service or emails; can be a brochure, a newsletter or other type of written appeal |
| **Grants:** Usually done through a written request to a foundation, government or other funder |
| **Leadership Giving Program**: A formalized program that recruits and recognizes donors who make contributions above a certain giving level. The Alexis de Tocqueville Society, available through United Way, is an example of a leadership giving program for givers of $10,000 or more |
| **Membership Campaign:** An annual effort to solicit funds from the membership; includes an emphasis on giving as a requirement in a church or association, for example |
| **Personal Ask**: One-on-one ask of targeted individuals for a specific donation of equipment, time or money |
| **Planned Giving**: A structured program within a nonprofit or foundation which focuses on the development of giving strategies for current and future donors based on the individual's wealth; can include charitable remainder trusts, naming |

| |
|---|
| the nonprofit in a will, or a wide variety of other estate planning strategies, including starting a foundation |
| **Product Sales:**  Involves the development, marketing and sales of specific products, with the proceeds benefiting the nonprofit;  Particularly valuable in nonprofits with programs that include products made by participants (such as schools, child care, workshop for the disabled, thrift shop which trains workers, etc.) |
| **Social Media:** <br> Although not a primary fundraising strategy, strategies like Facebook, Twitter and LinkedIn provide opportunities to develop relationships with potential donors |
| **Telephone/TV:**  Uses the telephone or television to solicit donations either through an annual event (like a telethon), regular publicized events, or by paying for a fundraising firm to do ongoing asks |
| **Web Sites:**  Involves development of a web site on the internet that allows donors to read about the nonprofit and to make donations |

## Addendum D - Risk Management Audit

| Category | Standard |
| --- | --- |
| Insurance | Insurance needs of the nonprofit are evaluated annually |
| | Directors and Officers liability insurance is included in the budget |
| | The state's Good Samaritan laws and any relevant federal laws on volunteer liability are evaluated at least every other year to verify compliance |
| Abuse | Criminal background checks are conducted on all staff and volunteers (at local, state and federal databases) |
| | All staff, volunteers and clients (when appropriate) are trained on how to recognize and respond to abuse, bullying and sexual harassment |
| Cyber security | At least annually a data security expert reviews the nonprofit's vulnerability to hacking |
| | Annual inventories are conducted of all data devices, software and hardware |
| | Policies and procedures are established on use personal use of the nonprofit's electronic equipment, the network, internet, and changing of passwords |
| | Policies and procedures are |

| | |
|---|---|
| | established on budgeting, updates and maintenance of hardware and software |
| | Policies and procedures are established on off-site backups of critical donor, volunteer, client and staff personal data |
| | Policies and procedures are established on access to confidential client, donor, volunteer and staff data |
| | Cyber security is included in the annual budget |
| Health and Safety | Staff and volunteers are trained on the proper use of all equipment |
| | Staff and volunteers are trained on how and when to report injuries |
| Disaster Plans | An internal disaster plan outlines how the nonprofit will respond to disasters (man-made or external) which affect the nonprofit's ability to achieve their mission and/or serve clients |
| | The internal disaster plan has been reviewed and approved by local emergency responders |
| | Staff, clients and volunteers have been trained on how to deal with an internal disaster and understand the chain of command |
| | Emergency supplies and equipment are stored on premises |

| | |
|---|---|
| | and checked annually to make sure they are still useable (such as fire extinguishers) |
| | Emergency telephone numbers (responders, staff, board and volunteers) are easily accessible to everyone |
| | Emergency contact numbers for client family numbers are easily accessible to the appropriate individuals. |
| | The internal disaster plan includes how the nonprofit will assess the impact of the internal disaster on the nonprofit's staff, clients and volunteers. |
| | An external disaster plan has been developed which outlines what role the nonprofit will play in any disasters impacting the community |
| | Mutual Aid Agreements or Memorandums of Understanding have been signed with emergency responders you have agreed to work with in the event of an external disaster |
| | Volunteers and staff have been trained by emergency responders on their duties in the event of an external disaster |
| | The external disaster plan includes how the nonprofit will assess the impact of the external |

| | |
|---|---|
| | disaster on the nonprofit's staff, clients, volunteers and the community |
| Crisis Communication | The risk management committee has identified potential scenarios which could require implementation of the crisis communication policies and procedures |
| | Written policies and procedures have been developed which identify who will respond to media inquiries and when in the event of a crisis |
| | Policies and procedures indicate how board members, staff, volunteers, clients, donors and other stakeholders will be informed about the crisis |
| Contingency Funding | The Finance Committee has recommended to the board the minimum and maximum amounts needed (i.e. 6 months of income) to insure the financial viability of the nonprofit |
| | The board has approved the establishment of a restricted contingency fund and the fund is reserved for only board-approved expenditures in emergencies (such as failure to receive a long-standing grant, internal disaster, etc.), with all expenditures approved by the board of |

| | |
|---|---|
| | directors |
| | The Finance Committee has developed a method to add money to the fund over a designated period until it reaches a specific threshold and will develop policies related to investment of funds |
| | No more than 20% of funding for the nonprofit comes from any single source with this analysis occurring annually as part of the strategic planning process |

## Addendum E

## Risk Management Policies

| Insurance Policies |
|---|
| 1.  The board of directors will purchase D&O insurance. |
| 3.  The administration committee will annually review insurance packages currently in use and determine if additional insurance is needed, making recommendations to the board.  The staff will assist by doing a preliminary analysis and presenting it to the committee |
| 4.  Adequate insurance coverage will be included in the annual budget. |
| 5.  The state's Good Samaritan laws and federal laws will be checked at least every other year to verify the nonprofit complies. |
| **Abuse Prevention Policies** |
| 1.  All staff and volunteers working with vulnerable clients will be trained on how to recognize abuse. |
| 2.  Staff or volunteers accused of abuse will be suspended until the allegations are investigated by the proper legal authorities and the individual is cleared or criminal charges are filed.  If cleared, the individual will be restored to employment and receive back pay for the suspension period.  If charged, the individual will be fired and receive no back pay. |
| 3.  Criminal background checks will be conducted on all staff and volunteers working with vulnerable clients. |
| 4.  All new staff and volunteers will be paired with an experienced person for the first year of their |

| involvement. |
| :--- |
| **Health, Accessibility and Safety** |
| An employee committee will be established by the ED. |
| The committee is responsible for finding and reporting any items that need to be replaced or repaired. |
| The board of directors will include in the annual budget line items for facilities and equipment maintenance, repair and replacement. |
| The committee will develop training programs that will encourage healthy lifestyles for clients, staff and volunteers. |
| **Disaster Readiness** |
| The employee health and safety committee will be responsible for developing the internal disaster plan and procedures. |
| In the event of a disaster at the facility, the ED or designee will implement the board-approved plan and notify the board chair as soon as possible. |
| In the event of a disaster in the community, the nonprofit will implement the board approved external disaster plan and notify the board chair as soon as possible |
| In the event of any crisis, only the board chair and ED are authorized to speak to the media on behalf of the nonprofit. Should they not be able to do so, the associate ED and vice chair of the board will speak on behalf of the nonprofit. |
| Before speaking to the media, the spokespersons will confer and develop written responses to the crisis. Such responses will occur within 24 hours of the crisis, or as quickly as possible. |

| Cybersecurity |
| --- |
| At least annually, a data security expert will review the organization's vulnerability to hacking |
| Annual inventories will be conducted of all data devices |
| The number of people with access to the organization's network will be limited to senior staff |
| Passwords for all networks and computers will be changed monthly |
| All software will be updated quarterly |
| All data will be backed up daily, both with a hard copy stored off-site and on the Cloud |
| Access to confidential client and employee data will be on a secure site, and accessible only to designated supervisors |

# Resources

https://mailchi.mp/lp-associates/covid19-1642409?e=029d2215ca

https://www.nonprofitpro.com

Southerlyn.Reisig@uww.unitedway.org

https://www.nonprofitquarterly.org

https://www.flnonprofits.org/page/Coronavirus

https://independentsector.org/covid19/

https://www.fema.gov/

## About the Author

Marilyn L. Donnellan, MS, has more than 40 years'
 experience as a nonprofit CEO and consultant. The nonprofits where she served ranged in size from a single staff organization with a budget of $150,000 to a $6 million nonprofit with 300 staff. Her knowledge of disaster readiness and response is based on assisting with developing plans at the local, state and federal level. She is the author of numerous articles in nonprofit trade journals and her books on nonprofit management are in use in more than a dozen countries. She is the author and presenter of dozens of webinars and webeds. She has a Bachelor's degree in Human Resources Management and a Master's degree in Administration

### Other Books by M. L. Donnellan, MS

- *The Complete Guide to Church Management* (English),
  www.amazon.com/author/mldonnellan
- The *Nonprofit Management Simplified* series on*: Internal Operations*, *Board and Volunteer Development*, and *Programs and Fundraising*
- *The Nonprofit Toolkits*
  www.amazon.com/author/mldonnellan

**Connect with the Author**
mldonnellanauthor@gmail.com
www.mldonnellan.com